Flo Rida

by C.F. Earl

Superstars of Hip-Hop

Alicia Keys

Beyoncé

Black Eyed Peas

Ciara

Dr. Dre

Drake

Eminem

50 Cent

Flo Rida

Hip Hop:
A Short History

Jay-Z

Kanye West

Lil Wayne

LL Cool J

Ludacris

Mary J. Blige

Notorious B.I.G.

Rihanna

Sean "Diddy" Combs

Snoop Dogg

T.I.

T-Pain

Timbaland

Tupac

Usher

Flo Rida

by C.F. Earl

Mason Crest

Flo Rida

Mason Crest
370 Reed Road
Broomall, Pennsylvania 19008
www.masoncrest.com

Printed and bound in the United States of America.

First printing
9 8 7 6 5 4 3 2 1

Library of Congress Cataloging-in-Publication Data

Earl, C. F.
  Flo Rida / by C.F. Earl.
     p. cm. – (Superstars of hip hop)
  Includes index.
  ISBN 978-1-4222-2525-7 (hardcover) – ISBN 978-1-4222-2508-0 (series hardcover) – ISBN 978-1-4222-2551-6 (softcover) – ISBN 978-1-4222-9227-3 (ebook)
  1. Flo Rida–Juvenile literature. 2. Rap musicians–United States–Biography–Juvenile literature. I. Title.
  ML3930.F57E27 2012
  782.421649092–dc22
  [B]
                                    2011005803

Produced by Harding House Publishing Services, Inc.
www.hardinghousepages.com
Interior Design by MK Bassett-Harvey.
Cover design by Torque Advertising & Design.

Publisher's notes:
• All quotations in this book come from original sources and contain the spelling and grammatical inconsistencies of the original text.
• The Web sites mentioned in this book were active at the time of publication. The publisher is not responsible for Web sites that have changed their addresses or discontinued operation since the date of publication. The publisher will review and update the Web site addresses each time the book is reprinted.

DISCLAIMER: The following story has been thoroughly researched, and to the best of our knowledge, represents a true story. While every possible effort has been made to ensure accuracy, the publisher will not assume liability for damages caused by inaccuracies in the data, and makes no warranty on the accuracy of the information contained herein. This story has not been authorized nor endorsed by Flo Rida.

Contents

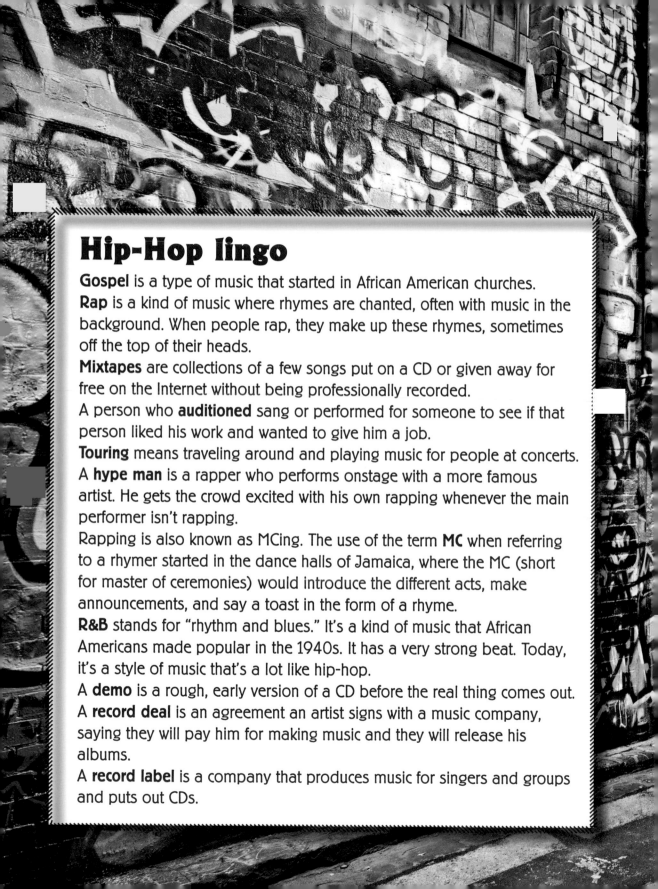

Hip-Hop lingo

Gospel is a type of music that started in African American churches.

Rap is a kind of music where rhymes are chanted, often with music in the background. When people rap, they make up these rhymes, sometimes off the top of their heads.

Mixtapes are collections of a few songs put on a CD or given away for free on the Internet without being professionally recorded.

A person who **auditioned** sang or performed for someone to see if that person liked his work and wanted to give him a job.

Touring means traveling around and playing music for people at concerts.

A **hype man** is a rapper who performs onstage with a more famous artist. He gets the crowd excited with his own rapping whenever the main performer isn't rapping.

Rapping is also known as MCing. The use of the term **MC** when referring to a rhymer started in the dance halls of Jamaica, where the MC (short for master of ceremonies) would introduce the different acts, make announcements, and say a toast in the form of a rhyme.

R&B stands for "rhythm and blues." It's a kind of music that African Americans made popular in the 1940s. It has a very strong beat. Today, it's a style of music that's a lot like hip-hop.

A **demo** is a rough, early version of a CD before the real thing comes out.

A **record deal** is an agreement an artist signs with a music company, saying they will pay him for making music and they will release his albums.

A **record label** is a company that produces music for singers and groups and puts out CDs.

Chapter 1

Spotlight on Flo Rida

Today, Flo Rida is one of rap's biggest hit makers. His music is on the radio, on TV, in movies, and in clubs. Songs like "Low" and "Right Round" have made him a star.

Flo Rida wasn't always a star, though. He's worked hard to get where he is. When he started in music, he was just a young man with a dream living in Miami.

Early Life

Flo Rida's real name is Tramar Dillard. He was born on December 16, 1979.

Tramar was born in Carol City, Florida. Carol City is a neighborhood of Miami. Growing up, Tramar lived in the 187th Street Projects. His mother raised him. She and Tramar's father split up when he was very young.

Tramar had seven sisters. His mother raised all eight of her children on her own. Tramar's father wasn't completely out of his son's life. But Tramar grew up mostly with his sisters and mother. He was the only boy in the house.

Carol City was a very tough neighborhood. Tramar's mother always told her children to stay out of trouble. She told them that even if they lived in a rough place, they didn't have to become rough

Flo Rida grew up in a Miami neighborhood called Carol City. The neighborhood wasn't always the best place to grow up, but it helped to shape Flo Rida into the person he is today.

themselves. Tramar took these words to heart. He knew friends who got into trouble. Some even went to jail. But Tramar always chose a better path. He remembered what his mother taught him. He did his best to make the right choices.

Music helped Tramar stay out of trouble. Tramar's father was a musician. And though he wasn't always around, he did support Tramar's love of music. He always told Tramar to express what he felt and thought through music.

Tramar's sisters were also a big part of the music he listened to growing up. His sisters would show Tramar all sorts of different music. Some of his sisters even formed their own **gospel** group.

Though Tramar loved many different types of music, he loved **rap** more than any other. Soon, Tramar was rapping with friends. He spent time making **mixtapes** in his aunt's garage. He got better and better at rapping and making music.

When Tramar was in the ninth grade, he had a chance to rap with a group. The group was called The Groundhoggz. The group was looking for new members. Tramar **auditioned** for them and joined right away.

The Groundhoggz started making music together. They had concerts around Miami. Tramar was on his way to making it as a rapper. Even though his dreams were still a long way off, he had his start in music.

A Chance at a Dream

Then the Groundhoggz played a show that really helped Tramar move toward his rap dreams. The group had a concert with the rapper Scarface. A friend of the rapper Fresh Kid Ice was at the show. He saw Tramar's skill. He knew that Tramar had talent and needed a break. He told Fresh Kid Ice about the young Miami rapper.

Fresh Kid Ice had been a member of the group 2 Live Crew. Now, he was **touring** the country. He needed a **hype man** to come to Hawaii. He decided he'd take Tramar. At eighteen years old, Tramar was headed to Hawaii as a hype man for a famous rapper. This was a great chance for him.

As hype man, Tramar had to get the crowd into Fresh Kid Ice's concerts. The hype man's job is to add to an **MC**'s show. He has to get people excited about the MC he's hyping. The hype man is meant to make the show as much fun as possible.

When Tramar was done touring with Fresh Kid Ice, he got another big break. DeVante Swing, a singer with the '90s **R&B** group Jodeci, noticed Tramar on tour. He asked for a **demo** of his music. When Swing heard Tramar's music, he told the Miami rapper to fly to Los Angeles right away. The next day, Tramar was on a plane. He was headed to L.A. to make his music dreams come true.

Tramar in Los Angeles

Tramar was ready to start his life in music. He was going to be working with an R&B legend. DeVante Swing wanted to see Tramar get a **record deal**. He wanted to make sure Tramar could get his music out. Swing saw that Tramar had talent for rap. He saw that Tramar could be the next big thing in rap music.

While in Los Angeles, Tramar worked on making sure his music was as good as it could be. He soaked up the style of California's music. He listened to new sounds. They helped him shape his own music.

Tramar also learned about different styles of hip-hop music from all over the country. He studied Southern rap. He learned about East Coast rap. He listened to rap from the Midwest. Tramar saw that rap and hip-hop were different all over. He started to pull different sounds into his own music, making it even better.

Tramar spent years in Los Angeles trying to make it. Many record labels call the big California city home.

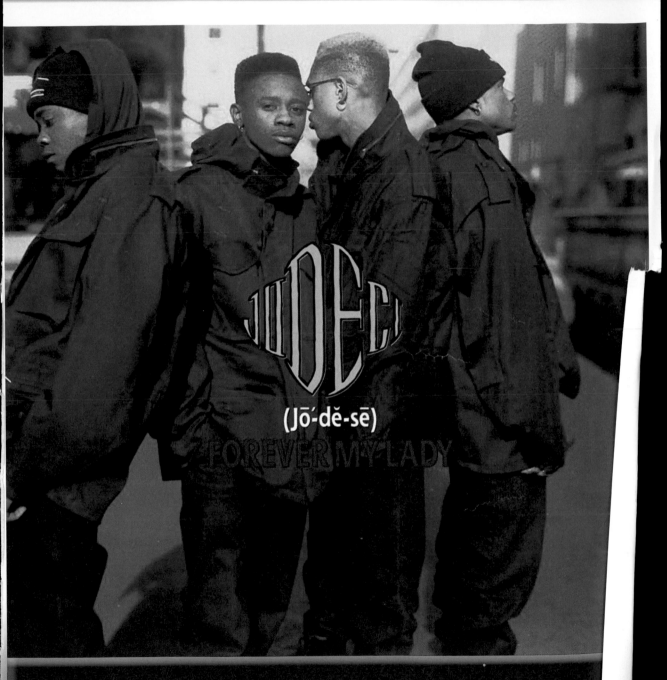

DeVante Swing sang in the popular R&B group Jodeci. He knew that Flo Rida's music could be successful, and he worked hard to help Flo get a record deal in Los Angeles for years.

In L.A., Tramar had to struggle to get his music heard. He and DeVante went to many of the biggest **record labels**. They went to Death Row Records. The famous label was once home to Tupac, Dr. Dre, and Snoop Dogg. Tramar and DeVante went to the most of the big record labels in L.A. But they all said they didn't want to put his music out.

Tramar worked hard to get out his music. He'd hit the streets, putting his mixtapes into people's hands. He was reaching for his dreams. And he was so close! L.A. was one of the biggest music cities in the world. Some of the biggest record companies in the world were based in L.A. Some of rap's biggest stars had come from the city. Now, Tramar was working hard to follow in their footsteps. But it was a tough path to take. Tramar was doing all he could, but it didn't seem to be paying off the way he'd hoped.

Tramar stayed in L.A. with DeVante Swing for four years. He couldn't get the record deal he wanted, though. He learned a lot about music from Swing, though. He learned a lot by looking at hip-hop's many different styles. His music got better and better. But without a deal, Tramar couldn't reach the heights he and Swing wanted.

Tramar had tried to make his dreams come true. He'd gone to Los Angeles to make it in music. Now, he was headed home. He wasn't giving up. But he knew he needed to take a break from the music world. Even if it was just for a little while.

Hip-Hop lingo

An **album** is a group of songs collected together on a CD.

Chapter 2

After Los Angeles

After trying so hard to get a record deal in L.A., Tramar needed to try something else. He thought hard about what his next move would be. He decided he should continue his education. So Tramar headed off to college.

Going to College

Tramar ended up going to the University of Nevada, in Las Vegas. While there, he studied international business.

Tramar understood how important education was to being successful. Later, he said that even though he didn't know it at the time, college would help him in his music career. While Tramar was going to college, he wasn't sure what he wanted to do yet. He knew he liked business and wanted to make music. But he wasn't sure how one could be mixed with the other. It took a while before he understood that his education only helped him in the music world.

"To everyone . . . who's trying to do music or anything, it helps to have even just a little school," Tramar said later. Now he tells his fans

FRANK & ESTELLA BEAM HALL

Tramar went to the University of Nevada in Las Vegas to study business.
Tramar has said that his education helped his career as Flo Rida.

that education is important to be your best—whatever you want to do. Education is a way to reach your dreams, even if it doesn't seem like it at the time.

After finishing college at the University of Nevada, Tramar started going to Barry University. In 2006, after he'd been going to Barry for only two months, he got an important call. A Miami record label wanted to talk to him about his music. They thought he had a lot of talent. They also saw that he needed a break to take his music to the next level.

Soon, Tramar was ready to chase his dreams again. This time, he knew he wouldn't stop until his dreams came true.

Another Shot

In Miami, Tramar started working with a record label called Poe Boy Entertainment. Poe Boy was focused on putting out artists from Miami. They wanted to build up Miami as a center for hip-hop music. They saw that Tramar could be a big part of Miami's rap scene.

Tramar started performing under the name Flo Rida. His home state was an inspiration for his name. But his name was also based on the way he rapped. Flo Rida's style was smooth. He could rap fast or slow. No matter the beat, he'd find the right flow for it.

Soon, Flo Rida was making connections with other artists. He put out a song called "Birthday" with rapper Rick Ross. Rick Ross also worked with Poe Boy Entertainment. Like Flo Rida, Ross was from Miami.

Next, Flo Rida worked with DJ Khaled. Khaled was working on an **album** called *We The Best*. He called in Flo Rida to rap on a song called "I'm from Dade County." Dade County was also known as Miami-Dade County. Miami was in Dade County.

Working with Rick Ross and DJ Khaled helped to make Flo Rida a star.
Like Flo, both Ross and Khaled come from Miami.

"I'm from Dade County" was the first big song for Flo Rida. The song featured rappers Trick Daddy, Trina, Rick Ross, Brisco, Dre, and C-Ride. These Miami rappers came together to make a song for their city. Many of them had worked with Poe Boy Entertainment, too. The close group of Miami artists wanted to see their city on the hip-hop map. They wanted the world to know that Miami was putting out great hip-hop music. With many big artists on the song, and DJ Khaled behind it, people who'd never heard of Flo Rida got to hear him rhyme.

In 2007, a year after he came back to Florida, Flo Rida got his biggest break in music yet. With Poe Boy Entertainment's help, he signed a record deal with Atlantic Records. Atlantic was one of the biggest labels in music. Flo had tried to sign with labels like Atlantic when he was in L.A. with DeVante Swing. Back then, he hadn't had any luck. But now, Atlantic was ready to put his music out. They finally saw what Flo knew all along. He had talent and drive. Flo Rida knew he could make it in the rap world. There was no stopping Flo Rida now.

Hip-Hop lingo

A **single** is a song that is sold by itself.

The **hook** of a song is a short section that catches people's attention. A lot of times, the hook is the chorus, but not always.

The **singles chart** is a list of the best-selling songs for a week.

A **soundtrack** is a collection of all the songs on a movie.

Producers are the people in charge of putting together songs. A producer makes the big decisions about the music.

Billboard is a magazine that keeps track of which songs are most popular.

Each year, the National Academy of Recording Arts and Sciences gives out the **Grammy Awards** (short for Gramophone Awards)–or Grammys–to people who have done something really big in the music industry.

When someone has been **nominated**, he has been picked as one of the people who might win an award.

A **collaboration** is when two or more people work together on a project.

Chapter 3

Flo Rida Goes Worldwide

After signing with Atlantic Records, Flo Rida was ready to take on the music world. He started working on his first album. Before it was out, though, he'd have one of the biggest rap songs of the decade.

"Low"

On September 16, 2007, Flo Rida put out the first **single** from his first album. The song was called "Low." T-Pain sang the **hook** on the song.

By November, "Low" had made it into the top hundred on the **singles chart.** The song reached number one by the start of January 2008. "Low" was at number one on the singles chart for ten weeks. The song stayed in the top ten for twenty-three weeks.

In February 2008, "Low" came out on the **soundtrack** to the movie *Step Up 2: The Streets*. "Low" was also played in all the ads for the movie. People heard the song on TV who might not have heard it otherwise.

"Low" was a huge hit. It was on the radio, on TV, and in a movie. In early 2008, the song seemed to be everywhere. It was helping Flo

"They say if you grind hard enough, you'll shine," Flo Rida told an interviewer, talking about the success of "Low." "It's the greatest feeling in the world."

Flo Rida had reached his dreams of making it in music. He had one of the biggest songs of 2008. His album had sold hundreds of thousands of copies. His music was known around the world. A few years before, Flo Rida didn't know if he'd ever get his chance in music. By the end of 2008, he'd reached heights most artists never do. He was one of rap's newest, most popular stars.

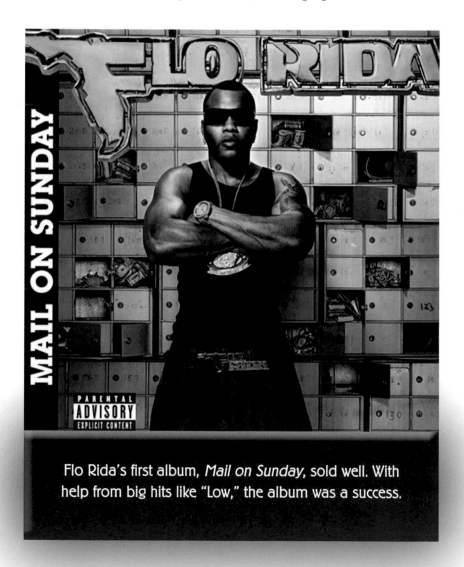

Flo Rida's first album, *Mail on Sunday*, sold well. With help from big hits like "Low," the album was a success.

Working with Other Artists

After the success of "Low" and *Mail on Sunday*, Flo started working with more artists. He got to make songs with some of the biggest artists in music.

Flo Rida worked on the remix of "4 Minutes" by Madonna. He worked with Lady Gaga on a song called "Starstruck." He worked with Rick Ross again on a remix of Ross's "Speedin."

Flo Rida also helped an Australian R&B singer named Jessica Mauboy on a song called "Running Back." The song was a huge hit in Australia. It won many awards and sold very well. It was one of the biggest songs of 2008 in Australia.

With hits like "Low" and "Running Back," Flo Rida wasn't just popular in his home country. He was known around the world. His music had touched people across the globe. Many artists dream of being successful in one country. Flo Rida was successful in many.

Working with other artists had helped Flo Rida become even more popular. Artists really wanted to work with him after *Mail on Sunday*. They saw that he brought a lot to a song. Artists wanted his help in making songs that could be as big as "Low."

The year 2008 was a big one for Flo Rida. He'd gone from having no luck in music to having one of the biggest songs of the year.

Flo Rida's R.O.O.T.S.

Mail on Sunday had made Flo Rida a star. His single "Low" was a big hit. Flo knew he needed to keep things going, though. He started working on his next album right away. A little more than a year after *Mail on Sunday*, Flo Rida was ready to put out his second album. He called it *R.O.O.T.S.* The name stands for "Route Of Overcoming The Struggle." The name means a lot to Flo Rida. He'd done a lot to get where he was. He'd worked for years to make it in music.

Flo Rida recorded *R.O.O.T.S.* in 2008. He worked with many famous artists on the album. Akon, will.i.am, Wyclef Jean, Ke$ha, Ne-Yo, and Nelly Furtado all worked on songs for *R.O.O.T.S.* will.i.am, Stargate, Jim Jonsin, and Travis Barker all helped produce on the album.

The first single from *R.O.O.T.S.* was called "Right Round." The song featured singer Ke$ha. Ke$ha's name only appeared on the song outside the United States, though. "Right Round" was a giant hit. The song reached number one on the singles chart in the United States. It was also a hit in countries across the world. "Right Round" topped the charts in Australia, Canada, Ireland, and the UK.

"Right Round" showed people that Flo Rida could be more than just "Low." That song had helped him become a famous artist. "Right Round" proved he deserved the fame. Flo Rida was now known for making big hit songs. His music kept people dancing and having a good time.

After "Right Round," Flo Rida put out four more singles from *R.O.O.T.S.* The second single was called "Shone." The song made it to number fifty-seven on the singles chart. The next single was called "Sugar." "Sugar" featured singer Wynter. "Sugar" was a top-ten hit, making it the second from *R.O.O.T.S.* It reached number five on the singles chart.

Flo Rida's fourth single from the album was called "Jump." Singer Nelly Furtado sang the hook. "Jump" made it onto the Hot 100 chart. It was also a hit in Canada and Australia. The last single from *R.O.O.T.S.* was called "Be On You." Ne-Yo helped Flo Rida on the song. "Be On You" made it all the way to number nineteen on the singles chart.

R.O.O.T.S. was a success. In its first week out, it sold 55,000 copies. That week, the album was number eight on the albums chart.

After becoming famous with "Low," Flo Rida kept making big hits with songs like "Right Round" and "Sugar." Flo also kept working with some of music's biggest stars.

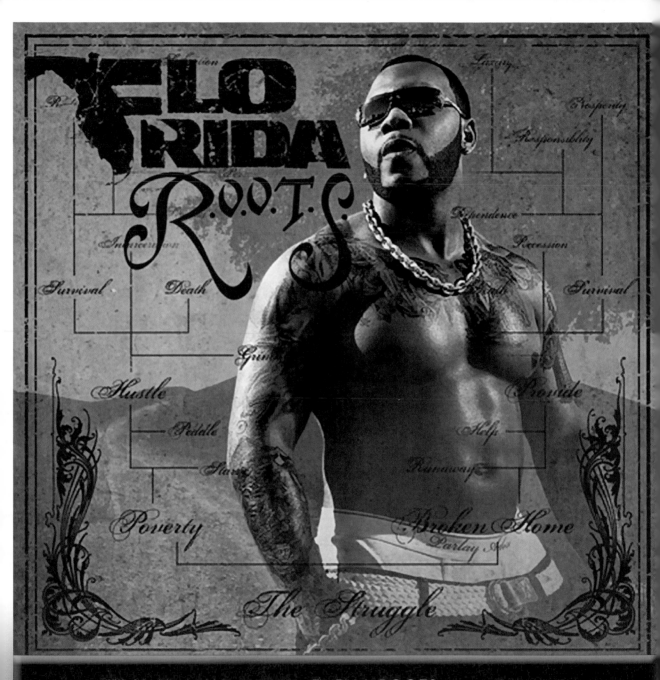

With big hits and big guest stars, Flo Rida's R.O.O.T.S. was another success for the Miami rapper. "Right Round" with Ke$ha was a hit around the world, helping the album to sell more.

By the end of 2009, the album had sold around 247,000 copies in the United States alone. *R.O.O.T.S.* was the eighth-best-selling rap album of the year.

Across the globe, *R.O.O.T.S.* sold more than half a million copies. It didn't sell as well as Flo Rida's singles, but many artists only dream of selling as many albums as Flo.

R.O.O.T.S. made it into the top ten on the U.S. album charts. On the Top Rap Album charts, it reached number three. It was also a hit around the world. The album reached the number-one spot on Australia's Urban Albums Chart. It also hit number one on the UK R&B chart.

R.O.O.T.S. was one of the top-ten highest selling rap albums of 2009. The album's hit singles had helped sales in a big way.

Near the end of 2009, Flo Rida learned he'd been nominated for a Grammy. At the 2010 Grammy Awards, Flo Rida was up for Best Rap Album for *R.O.O.T.S.* Flo was up against some of the biggest names in rap for the award. Eminem's 2009 album, *Relapse*, was nominated too. So were hip-hop legends like Q-Tip, Mos Def, and Common. Eminem ended up winning the award. Flo Rida was happy just to be among some of hip-hop's greats.

They year 2009 had been another big one for Flo Rida. Not only had he put out his own album, but he'd also worked on lots of music with other artists. And he wasn't done yet!

Hip-Hop lingo

A **beat** is the basic rhythm or pulse of a piece of music.

Someone who **inspired** a person gave her ideas and made her want to do something.

A **charity** is a group that gives time, money, or other things to help make people's lives better.

Chapter 4

Only One Flo Rida

Flo Rida was living his dream. He'd become the rap superstar he'd always wanted to be. With *R.O.O.T.S.*, he'd sold hundreds of thousands of albums. He'd also had hit singles from the album. He'd even been nominated for a Grammy.

It seemed as though Flo Rida could do no wrong. And he didn't plan on slowing down any, either. He'd put out two albums in two years. Now, he was ready to start on his third.

Only One Flo (Part 1)

In 2010, Flo Rida began work on his third album. He wanted to make it something special. He wanted to try something new. He decided to split his third album in half. The first half would show his talent for making big hit songs. The second half would show his talent for rapping. The first part would be released in 2010. The second half would come out in 2011.

At first, the double album was called *The Only One*. The first half would be called *The Only One: Flo*. The second was supposed to be called *The Only One: Rida*. Soon, the name was changed to *Only One Flo*. The first half would be called *Part 1*, the second *Part 2*.

Flo Rida named the album *Only One Flo* for a few reasons. First, he wanted to say something about his place in rap. No one else, he thought, had the same skill with making catchy songs and catchy rhymes. But the title was also based on Flo Rida's childhood in Miami. Flo Rida was the only boy in the apartment where he lived with his mom and seven sisters.

Only One Flo (Part 1) came out on November 24, 2010. Flo Rida recorded the album in 2009 and 2010. The album featured Ludacris, David Guetta, Akon, and Gucci Mane, as well as others.

The first single from *Only One Flo (Part 1)* was called "Club Can't Handle Me." The song features French DJ David Guetta. Flo and Guetta met while performing at the same concert. The two hit it off and wanted to do a song together. Soon, Guetta emailed a **beat** to Flo and "Club Can't Handle Me" was born. When it came out as a single, the song was a hit. It reached number nine on the singles chart.

"Turn Around (5, 4, 3, 2, 1)" was the second single from *Only One Flo (Part 1)*. The song wasn't as big a hit as the first single, but it did well. It reached number ninety-eight on the singles chart.

In the UK, Flo Rida's song "Who Dat Girl" became a hit. The song featured singer Akon on the hook. The song reached number thirty-one on the UK R&B charts.

Only One Flo (Part 1) sold just 11,000 copies in its first week. The sales were very low for Flo Rida. He'd sold many more with his first two albums. But just as with his other albums, Flo Rida's singles did very well, even when his albums didn't. Flo Rida was still going strong, even if his album sales were low. Flo Rida had come a long way from Carol City, where he grew up.

In 2012, Flo Rida released *Wild Ones*. The album was first called *Only One Rida (Part 2)*, but Flo changed its name before putting it out.

Flo Rida's music is all about having a good time and feeling good. Hip-hop began in parties in New York City and today, Flo Rida is keeping the music fun and easy to dance to.

Flo Rida's "Feeling Good" features the voice of famous singer Etta James. James died in 2012.

Wild Ones had two hit singles. At the end of 2011, Flo Rida put out "Good Feeling." The single was a big hit. "Good Feeling" features singer Etta James. After she died in January 2012, Flo dedicated the song to her in a YouTube video.

The album's second single was called "Wild Ones." The song featured Australian singer Sia. Like "Good Feeling," the song was a hit. Flo Rida was proving that he could keep making hit songs.

Singles and Albums

"Low" is one of the best-selling songs of all time online. It has been downloaded more than five million times. *Billboard* even ranked the song as number three in their Hot 100 Songs of the Decade (2000–2009). *Billboard* also placed "Low" at number twenty-three in its All-Time Hot 100. In December 2007, "Low" was downloaded 467,000 times in one week.

In one week in February 2009, "Right Round" sold 636,000 copies online. Since it came out, the single has sold more than four million copies. "Sugar" was also very successful. The song has sold more than a million copies. "Club Can't Handle Me" also sold more than a million copies in the United States alone.

Flo Rida's albums haven't had the same success as his singles. Even though he's sold millions of singles, none of his albums have sold a million copies yet. Flo Rida doesn't mind that his albums haven't sold as well, though. While some might see this as a failing, Flo sees his high singles sales as a strength.

"You're trying to sell records, sell singles—do it all," he said. "The most important thing is . . . connecting with the fans on a worldwide basis."

Most artists only dream of having their songs become as popular as Flo's have. He's had hit songs all over the world. With two number-one songs and millions of single sales, he's not worried about what people think. He knows his fans love his music. His goal is to keep making hits for the whole world to enjoy.

International Music Group

In 2010, Flo Rida announced he'd started his own record label. He called the label International Music Group (IMG).

The first artist Flo Rida started working with was named Brianna. At eighteen years old, she was still young. But Flo Rida got his start in music early, too. He saw that Brianna could be the next big name in hip-hop. He said she was perfect for today's rap scene.

Flo Rida thought Lil Wayne and Nicki Minaj were good examples of what he'd like to do with his label. He said that Nicki Minaj's success proved to him that Brianna could make it big too. Lil Wayne had signed Nicki Minaj to his Young Money label. After joining Young Money, Nicki got very popular. Her first album, *Pink Friday*, sold very well. She was hip-hop's newest star. And in a music world without many female rappers, her success **inspired** others. Nicki showed rappers like Flo Rida that bringing more female MCs into the game could work.

Flo Rida was ready to start moving into the business of music with his IMG label. He'd been making his own hits and worked with other artists. But now it was time for him to start building hits for other rappers. Flo had studied business in college. Now, he was ready to mix his education and his music. International Music Group was giving Flo Rida a chance to become an even bigger success in music.

Big Dreams For Kids

Flo Rida didn't just work on music. He also started his own **charity**. The group was called Big Dreams For Kids. Flo Rida and a few others started the charity in 2009.

Nicki Minaj has become one of rap's biggest stars in recent years. Her success showed Flo Rida that his artist Brianna could have as big a career in music.

Flo Rida knows that with success comes responsibility. He knows that giving back is an important part of reaching your dreams. Flo Rida has made it big in music. He wants to make sure kids can chase their own dreams.

Flo Rida has had amazing success in the music world. The Miami rapper has come a long way from the Carol City neighborhood where he grew up.

Flo Rida said he started Big Dreams For Kids because of his own childhood. When he was a kid, he lived in a tough neighborhood. Carol City wasn't always safe for a kid. People Flo Rida knew as a kid got into some bad stuff. Some even went to jail. They made choices that the young Flo didn't agree with. He didn't want to get into trouble or follow his friends to jail. So, he turned his energy to music and sports. He played basketball and started making his own music. His neighborhood was tough. But he knew he didn't need to make the same bad choices others did. He could think for himself.

Big Dreams For Kids is all about letting kids know they can dream as big as they want. It's about telling kids they can make good choices. It's about helping kids understand just how great they can be. Flo Rida says you don't have to do what everyone else is doing. You can choose to makes something different out of your life.

Looking to the Future

Flo Rida has done some amazing things in just a few years. He's had hit singles. He's sold hundreds of thousands of albums. His music has been on the radio, on TV, and in movies. Flo Rida has done it all.

Flo has been making hit music for years. And there doesn't seem to be any signs he's slowing down. Flo's come a long way from the Carol City projects. Now, he's known around the world. Artists looking to make a club hit come to him for help. He's worked with some of the biggest artists of our time.

Flo Rida's albums may not have sold as well as he wanted. But he is always ready to come back with something new. He's had plenty of ups and downs in his life. He understands how to keep going, even when people say you can't do something. Flo Rida is not letting slow sales bring him, or his music, down.

Flo Rida continues to make the music his fans love so much. With *Only One Flo* and *Wild Ones*, Flo is still making big hits and selling albums around the world.

Many people wish they could make it big in music. Flo Rida made it happen. His hard work has paid off. No one can be sure what will come next for Flo Rida. Fans around the world wait for his new music. And he's ready to give the people what they want—more Flo Rida.

1979   Tramar Dillard (or "Flo Rida") is born on September 17, 1979 in Carol City, Florida.

1998   He graduates from high school. He begins his studies at the University of Nevada, Las Vegas.

2000   After two years of college, he returns home to pursue music full time.

2006   He signs to Poe Boy Entertainment. He takes the name Flo Rida, and begins teaming up with other artists, such as Rick Ross, Trina, T-Pain, and Trick Daddy.

2008   Flo Rida releases his first album, called *Mail On Sunday*.

The first single from *Mail On Sunday* is "Low." It stays at the number-one spot for longer than any other song that year.

Flo Rida appears as a guest on many other artists' albums. He appears on *We Global* by DJ Khaled, *Gutta* by Ace Hood, and *Starstruck* by Lady Gaga.

2009   Flo Rida's second album, *R.O.O.T.S.* comes out.

The single "Right Round" goes to number one on the charts.

He wins an award for Highest Selling Single (for "Running Back").

He wins the People's Choice Award for Favorite Hip-Hop Song (for "Low").

2010   Flo Rida's third album, *Only One Flo (Part 1)*, comes out.

"Club Can't Handle Me" is *Only One Flo*'s first hit single. It reaches number 9 on the charts.

He is nominated for a Grammy Award for Best Rap Album (for *R.O.O.T.S.*)

In December, Flo Rida creates his own label, called International Music Group.

2012   Flo Rida releases *Wild Ones*.

In Books

Baker, Soren. *The History of Rap and Hip Hop*. San Diego, Calif.: Lucent, 2006.

Comissiong, Solomon W. F. *How Jamal Discovered Hip-Hop Culture*. New York: Xlibris, 2008.

Cornish, Melanie. *The History of Hip Hop*. New York: Crabtree, 2009.

Czekaj, Jef. *Hip and Hop, Don't Stop!* New York: Hyperion, 2010.

Haskins, Jim. *One Nation Under a Groove: Rap Music and Its Roots*. New York: Jump at the Sun, 2000.

Hatch, Thomas. *A History of Hip-Hop: The Roots of Rap*. Portsmouth, N.H.: Red Bricklearning, 2005.

Websites

Flo Rida Official Website
www.officialflo.com

Flo Rida on AOL
music.aol.com/artist/flo-rida/albums

Flo Rida on MTV
www.mtv.com/videos/flo-rida/344332/right-round.jhtml

Flo Rida on MySpace
www.myspace.com/officialflo

Haitian Hip-Hop Fan Site
www.belrapkreyol.com

Discography
Albums

2008	Mail On Sunday
2009	R.O.O.T.S.
2010	Only One Flo (Part 1)
2012	Wild Ones

Index

About the Author

C.F. Earl is a writer living and working in Binghamton, New York. Earl writes mostly on social and historical topics, including health, the military, and finances. An avid student of the world around him, and particularly fascinated with almost any current issue, C.F. Earl hopes to continue to write for books, websites, and other publications for as long as he is able.

Picture Credits

Atlantic/Poe Boy Entertainment: pp. 24, 28, 40
Beyond the Barricade Photography: p. 27
Carrienelson1, Dreamstime.com: p. 37
Eva Rinaldi: p. 38
Featureflash, Dreamstime.com: p. 22
John K. Addis: p. 34
Ken Wood, Dreamstime.com: p. 18
Renjishino: p. 16
Robyn Mackenzie: p. 6
Sbukley, Dreamstime.com: pp. 1, 14, 20, 30
Thomas Pintaric: p. 12
Towpilot: p. 8
Uptown/MCA: p. 11

To the best knowledge of the publisher, all other images are in the public domain. If any image has been inadvertently uncredited, please notify Harding House Publishing Services, Vestal, New York 13850, so that rectification can be made for future printings.